THE SKY IS A GATE

The Sky is a Gate

Poems

BY

David Churchill

Pony One Dog Press
Washington, DC

THE SKY IS A GATE

© 2021 David Churchill

Cover art: "Float and Dream" by Dave White
Book layout: Barbara Shaw

ISBN 978-1-7322882-0-1

First Edition

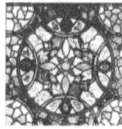

Published by:
Pony One Dog Press
Suite 113
1613 Harvard Street, NW
Washington, DC 20009

For PAM AND MARK STRANDQUIST,
the best Christians I know

Contents

DAVID CHURCHILL

The Sky is a Gate

The sky is not a wall but a gate
left swinging open by an unseen hand.

– W. Luther Jett, "And the Gate Opens this Way"

The Jesus Table

*The Son of Man is come eating and drinking; and ye say, Behold
a gluttonous man, and a winebibber, a friend of publicans and sinners!*

Luke 7:34

Here's the table where they sat,
here in the grape-leaf
shade of the trellis,
my longest table carried out,
my best wine poured,
my youngest running to serve with her sisters.

They took their seats as
each arrived, no separation made
between the sexes,
between gentile and Jew,
all mixed like beans and lentils,
chicory and onions in the one pot.

A tax-collector sat there,
a temple woman over and against him,
the usual people of the town,
even a Nubian merchant
on his way to the city,
and I heard no talk
of the kingdom of heaven that day,
for all the good cheer
that was there.

Then as a cloud out of Galilee
darkens the sun,
the laughter died
and starved men stood in the yard.
"Are you the one who is to come—
or should we seek another?"
Yea or nay, I can't recall . . .
But then they were gone,
and took no food or drink with us.

All this happened a long time ago.
The youngest is grown
with a daughter of her own.
We were saddened
by the news from the city,
but little time is left in our day
to puzzle or mourn,
and the city is far.

Still, we left the table here,
under the grape-leaves,
and when the grape-leaves stir,
shadow and sunlight play
across the wood
like it did that day,
and I swear I sometimes see
a touch of color in the shapes—

as I'm told you see
in the facets of a diamond,
in richer places
than our little town.

Michelangelo's Gallery of Ideas

Galleria dell'Accademia, Florence

I have never been to
the Galleria dell'Accademia
in Florence,
but I know it well.
It is a real-world model
of my personal psychology.

It is filled with statues
called *non-finito*,
which means unfinished in Italian,
struggling or waking figures
trying to get out
of their blocks of stone.

Some call them prisoners
and others slaves,
but I call them honest,
these forms
imbedded in marble,
revealing their sculptors
method of freedom.

The Galleria dell'Accademia
is one gallery
I don't have to visit.
I need only turn
to the people around me,

imbedded in spaces
that offer no resistance:

a man who feels
the world has mistreated him,
a child who looks
to his parents for justice,

a husband afraid
of his wife's passion,
and me—arguing
with a friend
who will never agree.

But why should we ever
think to be free—
stone-born and stone-dying?
How could stone
even conceive
of being free of itself?

So let them be.
Let them rest.
Let them sleep
till their sculptor returns.

Gothic Pandemic

Covid Pandemic, 2020

The images were shocking:
birds with hooked
or spearing beaks
in surgical gowns;
catfish whiskers,
goggles and shrimp-forks—
Hard to believe
one TV screen
could contain such sights.

The newspapers were worse,
full of holes:
piles of bodies
spilling through,
burning cities
and wagons full of bones—

And these holes were like
windows
impossible to close,
or turn off—

At least I could still read
the headlines:
tornadoes uproot
midwestern lives,
locusts in Africa,
Moroni dropping his trumpet . . .

Here we were only
wearing diapers on our faces
and the outdoors
was closed—

But one image
I couldn't get out of my mind:
a man with a lute,
ignoring it all—

Play, lute-man, play.
Play till the strings
grow through your fingers.
Let death find you
playing the lute.
Is it not but an uneasy sleep
after a too-rich meal?

DAVID CHURCHILL

A Case of Synchronicity According to Jung

Washington Hospital Center, 7/20/2020

This happened in the new room,
across the hall from the old
room, now wrecked;
where I had been born again
into a room where the mattress
was softer and a soft rain
lullabied against the window
and a gentler climate prevailed outside.
No violence of wind
or the breaking of eyes
and ears—
A room where the first thermals
of elation began.

My old room—where the epiphany
had unfolded itself
to a man who was soon
to join the ranks of the retired . . .
A good age to have an epiphany,
by itself, worth the cost.

There's not much to do
in a hospital bed,
if you are free of anesthetics,
and have need of review—
It was like a field
that unfolds under the first
tentative touches

of an unoccupied mind,
where one walks as if on a forest
trail, from vista to vista . . .

There like a spring rain
rinsing the soil from emerging shoots,
day-lilies in beds along the edges,
blue-bells and irises in beds
along the streams
and trees growing in rows,
a insight had occurred.

A fear well responded-to
doesn't have to be minded;
but a fear not minded
over a life-time
becomes a grave of fear,
shovelfuls of dirt deep,
until the grass grows green
again across the packed earth,
burying all the fear
of not being safe without a job—
I was, in short, afraid to be free.

My old old room—where
nothing to do crowded the small space,
till one finally found a seat
before the window to watch
the sky darken,

something volcanic come
gathering toward us,
and listen for the rain to begin,

and linger a little
as if in a well-groomed forest,
a well-earned rest,
among alleys of hickory and oak
as though one had already
forgotten
the intended diversion . . .
there, in front of the window,
watching the storm come—

THEN—rain.
Inside the window.
Pandemonium rain.
Panes dissolved, too weak to withstand.
Towels flung at the water.
Save everything you can.
Blinds blown in.
Klieg flash.
Locomotives colliding.

The new room
so calm it seemed
cut loose from the world,
bore me upward
on fluff of dandelion.

There will always be cancer
and there will always be storms.
There will always be
hidden motives and complexities,
things people have forgotten
that should never be forgotten,
like splinters under the skin
that *will* work their way out—

Still I don't know what it means,
if two things happening
together
is ever more than a coincidence . . .

All I know is
insight came softly
like moisture after a drought,
then a violence of weather,
inchoate —

And I am affected
whether I believe anything or not—
I am in the air
between peaks and the sky,
afraid of finding meaning
in the meaningless,
mistaken thinking leading astray.

We create meaning
in the world,
perceiving, thinking—
Yesterday something created meaning in me.

The Hills of Mount Pleasant

Mount Pleasant neighborhood, Washington DC 2020

It is hard to feel woeful
in a city,
but it happens—
Sometimes life
can drive you in a corner.
When it happens to me,
I go for a walk.

I walk in a neighborhood
near me,
where streets drive
through green tunnels
up and down,
and builders piled
dirt up behind stone walls
to set their houses
even higher.

The occupants rose and fell too
over the years.
Successful men
who built the first houses,
then renters jingling
keys to narrow rooms;
people more privileged
than me
now putter about in the shrubbery.

But the poor have
privileges too.
Mine is the privilege of walking.
Privileges are gifts
and my footsteps say
thank you
thank you thank you thank you.

All over this land the living
was good.
From the green hills
given out in grants
the size of whole countries
to the grain
rising itself
out of bottom-lands,
people took their blessings
for granted.

Next time around,
will I live
in one of these houses,
ceiling-fans on,
on already airy porches,
little cabinets
by the sidewalk,
full of romance novels
and children's books—

or will the police appear,
park
on the wrong side of the street,
want to get to know me?

Five Hundred Thousand Names

Covid Pandemic, May 28th, 2020

Man has been defined
so many ways.
Now he becomes
a builder of the void.

First thing to do
to bring order to the void
is to count it.
How many is the void?

Next thing to do
is to give it a name.
How long will it take
to say the name of the void?

Man means well but
sometimes he can't do it.
The void keeps growing.
How can we fill it?

Call on the God of Snow.
He names every flake
that falls to the ground.
Sometimes blizzards
cover whole continents;
alas, no two names are alike.

Love in a Time of Pandemic

Had we but world enough, and time,
This coyness, Lady, were no crime . . .

— Andrew Marvell, "To His Coy Mistress"

Turn off the game show.
Are we not depressed enough
already?
Let's talk about each other,
you and I—
I wonder why it is
we never became any closer.

Compliments are not enough,
verbal tricks
to trap you into intimacy,
nor a shared appreciation
for the ways of our pets.
It seems our bonds
will be no more
than an interlocking laugh or two.

What is it anyway
that brings two people close?
I will be the first
to reveal a vulnerability to you,
if you reveal
a vulnerability to me,

for I already know
your greatest vulnerability,
you already know mine.
They are the same—
Let us confess them then,
to each other,
and let us be close.

Let us confess that this life
is the strangest of lives,
a cross between a stage
and an executioner's cart,
hemmed in by a scenery
that seems painted by children.
It sways when we move
and collapses beneath us.

But some things can't happen—
Elephants can't jump
and cats can't stay
in the place where you put them.
The condemned can't bond
over a date for execution.

They are not bonding
who stand on a winter plain
about a grave,
struggling to hold
in their hearts old words,

blown out like candle
in polar winds.

The echoes of that cult
that had death constantly before it
fall fadingly about us.
Its god was a god who died.
Its sign, the electric chair of its time.

Their day began
with a cloud in the east,
glories of hidden light
crowding the shadowed hills.
For us day begins
with a cloud on the heart
and a click of the human mechanism.

We two could concoct
a conspiracy to never speak
its name,
be like the world
that speaks only with its hands,
a language missing one word—
But each must deny it
separately and alone.

But we *should* be close,
reason or no—
Life can't help but be about itself.

Even that ancient cult
gathers not for the cloud
but the rays behind it.
That which is so opaque to us
may be no more
than the veil of a spider,
full of prisms in the morning.

No one can bond over death
because death continuously
passes into life—
So let us live, and make life,
and give our assent
to the power of something
that drives us the harder,
the more we resist.

Bucket Street

Irving and 14th St NW, Columbia Heights, Washington DC

It's a beautiful day and
young men are drumming
in an orchestra
of buckets
and the sunlight
is throbbing.

No doubt they are drumming
from an excess
of joy, and another
young man is
playing a trombone.

People in purple
and gold and a rack
of pamphlets
want to tell you what it's all about,
and a man tried to
paint it and is
propping up his paintings.

A tide of mechanical
toys is loose
across the sidewalk,
tinkling for joy—
One made a run for it
and fell off the curb.

The Persistence of Myth

If myths are persistent
it must be
because they were
the conspiracy theories
of their day—

But here, watching
mythological Americans
with their guns
and heritage flags,
I am face to face
with a theory
I don't understand.

This is the time
when I turn off the set,
and my mind,
like the leaves of the
touch-me-not,
turns in on itself,
and I prefer to escape
in a reverie.

I wonder what
it would be like
to be one mind with nature,
a ready-made
day-dream of its day,

light rains to fall
like flute solos,
the wind in the pines
like harp strings,
the sunset a hallelujah chorus,

and to be able to actually
see fear:
a pair of eyes
staring with singular intent.

—Something slams.
Trees close again
and the ground closes
and nature shuts
again behind its
display case of beauties,

leaving the feeling
of being alone
on the Serengeti after nightfall
loose in my chest.

What benefits a man
to see fear
and the fearful
separated,
to see death

and the killer,
two instead of one?

Is life improved
by doubling itself,
first knowing death,
then dying?

What does improve life
is staying busy.
Forget your lost
oneness with unknowing—
Be one mind in knowing.

Join us in feeding
the hungry,
curing the sufferers.
We will pick our babies
from menus
and we will never die.

We are building something
lofty here,
that already touched
the sky in conception,
a home for those
whose nature is to climb,
a separate pillar
of creation.

A cloud nudged
an inch
and a light blazed.
I am again
on my deck,

still trying to coax
rose-bushes
out of oak-tubs,
and an apple tree
in a planter,

the static of a radio
somewhere,
calling the faithful
to come,
fill stadiums.

The Fool

In the Rider-Waite Tarot deck and other esoteric decks made for
cartomancy, the Fool is shown as a young man, walking unknowingly
toward the brink of a precipice. He is also portrayed as having with him
a small dog. The Fool holds a white rose (a symbol of freedom from baser
desires) in one hand, and in the other a small bundle of possessions,
representing untapped collective knowledge. In occult tarot, he is one of the
22 Major Arcana, sometimes numbered as 0 (the first).

You can still see the image
in museums,
the old-style hero,
heart made pure
by prayer and fasting,
his lonely wanderings
dedicated
to aiding the wronged
and assisting damsels—

Long gone where all
fine heroes go,
etherealized into myth
and the pages
of comic books.
But his place remained,
an empty niche
in a cathedral wall.

Our "age demanded"
a new kind of hero,
a new wronged
and a new damsel,

and found them gathered
unaware on a hill:
a lunatic, a transvestite—
And a fool,
a child of the flower.

He would be a man who
fell too easily
under spells,
even spells that weren't
intended for him—
Like the spell cast
by the shadow
of leaves on a wall,
or a pattern of birds
on a sky,
and forgets where he is going . . .

His wanderings due
to a lack of order
in his inwardness,
like a land
where no roads connect,
and boundaries
as fragile
as bubbles on a soap-wand—

And he will be
a master

of everything passing,
and a lover of art,
and stand
before an antique frieze
and gaze at its figures
embedded in stone,

and hear from within
calling out
from their garlands
and beasts on parade
a voice crying,
'I bargained with life
for a few more years,'
and another crying,
'I expected to be rewarded
for being a good person,'
and will turn his back
on their certainties—

Others came too, each
bringing their own
measure of light,
till the morning
was raised in the sky—
Then after
what seemed like a lifetime,
taking their pieces

of the morning with them,
they left again,

and the sun, like
one rolling over in bed,
pulled what was left
into the ocean,
and a long slow
evening arrived,
replete with bird-song.

Morning found only
a string of love-beads,
a drifting of petals
on crushed grass
and a tear-drop of dew . . .

All of that multitude,
gone on their way—
The lunatic gone.
The transvestite gone.
The others, gone—

The Fool too left, finally,
last to leave.
While the others
loved the ones
they were with,

DAVID CHURCHILL

he fell in love with the sky,
a stairway of clouds
too high to be climbed,

but his eyes climbed,
and brought a vow
to their heights
for safekeeping:
I will build a mountain
in my heart,
and go there someday
for a view of the stars . . .

and for an aimless
life,
its precipice.

Spring Unseen

Covid Pandemic, 2020

In the book of seasons
some chapters are
missing,
like the Year Without Summer,
a time of hunger
and suffering,
but *this* season is missing
in a whole new way,

these pansies flickering
in April breezes,
these tulips trembling
in their Easter-basket green:
this is a season nobody sees.

People who didn't
plan gardens at all
had gardens grow anyway,
and many of those
wouldn't even have known—
till they glimpsed
from the safety of windows
solitary figures staring,
trying to name
every flower they saw.

Like junk at a curbside,
spring's pastels

seem to await
the resolution
of some municipal discomfort.

A man can live
in this country
without ever noticing
the palette
of each season is
different,
and that is no hardship—

But I will remember
this season a long time.
It may be the most beautiful
season I've seen . . .

Luna at the Window

The window is open,
the breeze through the screen
turning colder—
But the plants
at the window don't mind.

All day they have looked
from the edge
of an indoor forest,
moving their leaves
like children
waving their hands
in the stream of a hose—

A real breeze blows
out there,
and whole boughs swing
shaggy elbows,
cast real shadows
in a world
they have never been part of.

But I am not here
to feel sorry for plants.
They make no complaint.
They accept
their gallon of water,
never ask
for the intimacy of rain.

The other pets are asleep
on a soft blanket
on the couch,
and I am in the bedroom,
lying quietly
in the dark.

A different kind of world
is coming on
outside,
and I will stay a little longer
with Luna at the window.

Destroying Angel

Covid Pandemic, 2020

This is not like
the angel of the Lord who
flew over the roofs
of the people at midnight—
This is an angel who
goes under people
in daylight.

Like bubbles rising
to the surface where whales
are underneath,
fevers and coughing rise
to the surface
of the country around us.

People run
to where the bubbles appear,
try to contain it,
but it's always too late—
Whatever was there
is already gone.

It's a great time to go out
some people say.
Go to the restaurant,
likely you'll get in.
The angel passed me
and all I got was the sniffles.

Out there—
Beyond the window,
jonquils nod
in assenting brilliance;
celestial popcorn
on cherry trees,
behind invisible barricades.

I read in a book somewhere
about a pool in Jerusalem
by the gate
of the sheep,
where an angel of the Lord
came down
and stirred up the water.

So much of our lives
are in the hands of powers
we don't understand,
but for good
or for ill—
it should make us feel better.

Year Without Winter

Suddenly cherry blossoms
were blooming
and people began wondering
did they ever go away—

And the streets filled
abruptly with people
in shirt-sleeves
and people began wondering
where did they
come from?

And neighbors who once
had to shovel snow
off their cars
and had no place to put it,
forgot all about it,
and smiled at each other.

And people said
that's as good a reason
as any to be happy.
When life's good to people,
people are good
to each other.

Though I don't disagree,
I thought of all those ancients
who were going to

die this winter—
now have no choice
but to live another year . . .

I Grew Up in a Racist Country

I did not grow up in a racist country.
I grew up outside
a racist country.
But a country is a place
and a thing you harbor
inside you—

Black men drove cabs
on the docks of New York,
and opened doors
into lobbies rich
with smoke of cigars,
and their voices
were as strange
as curses in Moroccan souks.

Black boys ran
in alleys behind hotels,
smoked twigs snapped
from trees
and punched trash-can lids,
carried groceries
for tips and
loved to show white boys the ropes.

Black lives
lounged in crumbling houses,
stretched on gray couches
in dim rooms

.

glow-lit by televisions,
holes in walls
connecting obscure forms
to flickering lives.

I watched a drop
of piss in a toilet-bowl,
and wondered:
how does racism spread,
what medium
does it spread in,
and where does it go
when you no longer see it?
But physics is only
a part of the story.

White lives are
ship-board loves
with high-bred girls,
white-capped words
torn away by a wind
that still blows,
though you don't feel it:
'Come close to my lips.
I will tell you a secret.
It will make you feel special . . . . '

Ode to a Man who Drowned Swimming the Rio Grande, and his Daughter

June 26th, 2019

You, Oscar Martinez— there in the reeds,
you, with your daughter—
Did you not read our instructions?
This country wants only
the tired, the poor,
not swimmers of rivers.

The good people of this country,
the drivers of diesels,
the men waiting
for coal jobs to return
want only the tempest-tossed,
the huddled,
not parents with children.

You there, Oscar Martinez—
America is not a land
or a race or a religion.
America is a light
that has gone out
in the hearts of its people.

America is a river
that flushes down garbage,
contents of ash-trays

and drink cups.
Even its eddies
eddy in inner darkness.

Go home, Oscar Martinez,
take your daughter with you—
Go while the light
is still in you.

Wherein I Address the Problem of Suffering

I did not know, then,
how blessed I would be,
many years later,
but I should have known better—

There is no comfort
the living can offer
the dying.

So perhaps it was
more for myself
that I watched him pace
the impersonal room
in his golden slippers,
fretting like the child
he still seemed,

as though he already felt
the nurses tightening
their knots
on the trash bag
that would hold his remains
in a week,

and told him
suffering was energy
for change—

And for myself too
that in my mind
I stood at some nameless
siding and saw boxcars
covered in frost,
as if abandoned—
except for the padlocks,

and felt the weight
of a multitude
confined within,

and told them
it is through suffering
God draws us
to Him—

No—I comfort no one
with words.
I have no aid to give.
I come empty-handed
to suffering,

nor have I faith
the one who is suffering
will find sense
in his suffering.

It is like a shark-bite
in a fish-bowl,
the water reddens so quickly.
My happiness
turns its face away.

But I will not despair.
I will summon
the guard
to unlock the door of this car—

I will only despair
if there is no room
for one more.

Watching Rain Fall

Washington DC, July, 2019

We'd been getting warnings
all morning—
but when it came,
no one could see it,
the actual rain
in Pompeian gloom.

Streetlights were on,
Headlights twinkled brightly.
Everything shone,
like lights in a fish-bowl.

Walkways under water,
the roadways
were jumpier than frogs.
Puddles were trying
to return to the sky.

Only the trees were serene.
Their greenblack
boughs were the stuff of fairytales.
Through a dark forest
lights
were floating like fireflies.

Street Scene with Clouds

Mount Pleasant, September 12th , 2018

Here, where the alley
disembogues on the street,
pedestrians transform
in its mouth,
walk halfway and walk back,

is the bottom
of a chasm of clouds
like granite
over the roof tops,
a storm either coming
or going,
I couldn't tell—

The only thing missing
was a flock of Valkyries
like a handful of pepper,
blown between peaks—

Was *I* any more there
than the pedestrians passing,
who do not know
what occurs
in the trees sheltering their heads?

Or do I alone
lament the loss of a world
that leads into itself,
decry a world
that leads us away?

Under Lake Water

Lago di Brocciano, Italy, 1953

Under lake water,
like resting glass,
I found a wedding band,
hiding under a glint.

Sunken barges—
guarded by minnows,
secret shines
wink on sunfish scales,
too deep to reach.

Barely a decade
since blast-harried
figures passed,
filling this water
with useless ambitions.

But now we children
swam and played,
and prizes
were artillery-shells
and bubble-seeded grenades.

And when night fills
dreams
with uneasy peace,
bullet-riddled gleams
still light my sleep . . .

Pas de Deux with Bamboo

I watched the wind in the bamboo
across the alley
this morning,
that grows above the fence,
and a few stalks
that grow through,

and two stalks bowed
under the stalk-gray sky,
and swayed together,
and curtseyed to each other,
and bent back
to the ground
in their partner stalk's arms.

People jumped in their cars
and jerked away,
and another number
flicked into place
on the face of the clock;
still I remained,
stuck in my thoughts.

Everyone loves the feel
of a wind in
their hair,

but I want to know,
what is *this* wind
that makes bamboo sway,
and where can I find it?

The Afternoon of Christmas

The cats come out
from under the bed.
They do not sniff about
like dogs, but sit
as if wondering
what happened here.

Indeed there is much
to be wondered at:
chairs pushed about,
mugs and plates
in unaccustomed places,
wrapping-paper scraps.

Then it is time again
to finish that nap—
They depart as they came,
with the fanfare of cats.
They do not care
to make one get-together
out of the year
differently meaningful,

they do not care
to show they mean more
to each other
than they're able to say,
before another year passes . . .

Festival

Mount Pleasant, September 25th, 2011

I came out of our building
expecting to be blinded
by the sun:
instead someone had landed
a rainbow of trout,

and *I* was the swimmer,
eyelids exploding
in a river of color,
and every scale
was alive
as if struggling to breathe . . .

—Till a thunderstorm
occurred
and iridescent chaps
flowed past as
drummers advanced,
a parade in a sound-booth.

The whole south of the border
had come to our street,
aching playas where
there is no shade,
high altiplanos where
the wind plays the ocarina,

and the spine of the cactus—
That if one sticks you,
a street fills suddenly
with dancing vaqueros,
and images pour
like blood from your eyes.

To an Old Woman in a Wind with Umbrella

16th & Park Road NW, Washington DC

Street always bad, worst
backed-up block in the city,
short lifetime spent
watching lights change,
bodega-traffic passing,
smell of Cuban cigars,
Pho counters and Salvadorean
spiritual slave shops,

ending in the shadow
of the Sacred Heart,
holy pile of building blocks
hanging over the street,
engine of immobility
on Romanesque wheels—

Unless Ida Quadrille,
queen of bathroom bushes
and library naps,
is off her meds again—

"Don't think you foolin' me,
you heathens!
I know why God keepin' me
'round to the End Time—!"

—struggling up the ramp
to the locked doors,
tug of war with
Satan's chute
on the shopping-cart
behind her,
early for the dinner program . . .

Then a car goes and
you finally arrive
at a light that has waited for you—

And a voice on the
radio,
>   *"America will be saved,*
>   *in no time stadiums*
>   *will be definitely filled."*

Palmetto of the Morning

December is not a good month
for palmettos.

Night chills are cruel
to the blistering carapace
of Florida's swamps,
freeze up those multifarious legs

that kept them alive so long
their day is a geologic age,
and those two whiskers
like white canes

that can see danger better
than Judean prophets,
morning frosts stiffen
their tremulous feelings,

confuse them in their icy cracks,
their glittery safety under
frozen mulch—

Indoors too is cruel
to the sleeping carapace
wakened to jealous life,
—And O, so much life!

So many eons of striving
packed into one carapace,
upside down like a furious
eggbeater,
right-side up like a bottle-rocket,

and always with one thought:
inside—further inside—
away from the open hall—!
looking for safety
under the sole of any shoe.

But my shoe
will not be kind either,
—though it did not crush him.

The cats emerged
from their parallel universe,
and a bedroom door
opened softly behind me—

A great heaviness
fell over me then.
I felt all that life
in the palm of my hand,
in my protecting caress—

the way you want to hold
everything in life,

and a great heaviness
fell over my heart.

I put him down the garbage disposal.

Spring Day Through Windshield

Lafayette Circle, 5:30pm

A painter would say
the world is flat
when you look toward light,
so under rain clouds
that hide the sky,
the forsythia is deep.

A prayer-wheel multiplied
in banked glass
gives off sparks as
cars spin past,

their lights brush
the city's lost tourists,
tents of the homeless.

Lafayette plants his
back against the rush,
windshields string
with drops.
Some umbrellas are up.

Bull-Fighter of Cars

When I arrive at work
I look for my friend
who is already at work.
He is a bull-fighter of cars.

Their exhaust is his cape,
an intersection is his ring.
His suit of lights
is out, but
his motions ignite.

He goes down on
one knee and
cars hurtle to a stop—
He spins like a top and
cyclones cross.

I call him friend
but I don't know his name,
still he is a friend—
He teaches me how
to conduct my life.

Life at a Crossroads

I too went to the crossroads.
It was in rolling hills
and forest-cleared fields,
where Horsepen and Buckthorn
cross—
but you can find one anywhere,
and it doesn't always
have to be at night.

But there *will* always be
a man of sorts,
waiting for you there.
A man with a baseball cap
perhaps,
sitting by a table
with a watermelon on it . . .

'I seem to have lost
my way,' I said.
Which road will take me
home?'

'You know, don't you—?
Crossroads go
two ways at once.
I can tell you,
but when you arrive,
no one will know you.'

I thought then
of the value of things,
and those souls
whose lives
are a series
of crossroads,
whom everyone knows,
but have no home.

Dream of the Cat

My cat has a dream
and it's a recurring dream.
I don't know what it is
but I know what it's not:

it's not about food
or the litter in his box,
not about a chair
or the view from a window—

But when he has his dream
I know what it is,
and I leave off the tumbling
and drifting
of tumble-weed

and the jumping of jack-rabbits,
and sometimes roll over . . .
before returning to sleep.

The Cards of Madam Claire

Focus your attention.
Ignore the cold
gusting in every time
the door opens,
ignore the crowds
gusting in.
Ignore the table that tips
under our hands.
I will show you
your life in three cards.

You began as a builder.
Life handed you
the plans for a church.
You did the best
you could—
Pentangles of three
came together to help.

Card number two
is a confused and dark place:
earth and sea are
mixed up.
Even the moon
doesn't know
if its full or in crescent.

The eight of cups
that means emotion
are the only order
in this land—
But one cup is missing.
You are departing
to retrieve it.

What to make
of the last image?
Talk about what you see:
an angelic figure,
trading water
between grails,
signifying correspondence . . .

Apology to Christians

It happened in the second
half of the Sixties,
when I was vacationing in California
on a dollar a day—
I answered an ad
in a Los Angeles paper
and joined up with a group
of itinerant salesmen.

They drove all over the country
in a Volkswagen bug,
sleeping in motels
and eating at McDonald's,
and the highest salesman of all
was a girl with one leg,
and they sold
magazines door-to-door.

People we met
on the whole were pretty friendly,
in the lush
neighborhoods of Los Angeles,
and some even invited us in,
so you didn't mind
spending your days
among the palms and blue sky,
but no one
bought any magazines.

Finally the man
who gave us money for meals
said I'd trained
long enough—
Time to start earning my pay.
Next morning
before anyone was awake,
I picked my way
through the sleeping forms
across the floor,
and resumed my vacation . . .

I didn't leave a note—
But if I had,
it would have said this:
it feels so good
to be free,
to stand beside a road,
see where
the next ride takes you.
Thanks for the hospitality;
I follow a god without rules.

The Social Schedule of Death

*"My lords, would you like to hear a beautiful tale
of love and death?"*

> –J. Bedier, "The Romance of Tristan and Iseut"

If you're lost, you can look and you will find me, time after time

> –Cindy Lauper, "Time After Time"

Modern-Consciousness Man

I sit on the curb where Black lives matter,
a soldier for justice
and a seeker of truth,
hoping I can be here
without being noticed.

Someone stumbles on my foot.
The camera he holds
makes a bid for the ground.
Get out of the way
he says, can't you see
we're tryin' to make a film here?

I take his picture with my iPhone.

This has been a biblical year,
a time of fires and floods,
of hurricanes and plague—
And some people know why
and others don't know,
and when we look back
we will call it
a year of stumbling in the dark.

But some who would still seek God,
if there is one,
who have not found him in love;
seek him now in violence.
For the tempest

has come to our streets,
and I wish to feel terror
in the wrath of the tempest
if there is a God,
or feel nothing at all,
if there is none.

I have a name—but the name's not important.
I could be a medieval knight
or an accountant,
as long as no one knows who I am.
I am the same as
every man and every woman.
I am modern-consciousness man.

Yet modern-consciousness is nothing
but what we believe
in our present condition
humanity is.

Modern-consciousness man
has uncovered the powers
that shape mountains,
and left them for tourists,
and gone into space
and left that too for tourists.

Even alternate-reality man
goes to a doctor

to get his hemorrhoids checked.
When his ass hurts
it's a science-man he needs—

But sometimes it seems
we are only like children,
alone in an empty house,
thinking the house ours,
where all the counters are too high
and the chairs too big;

and alone in the too-big bed,
hearing the wind
whimpering through empty rooms
like a stray
who finally makes his way home,
finds his old masters gone,
like some family
of kindly giants no one believes in—

So I am many things but
one thing I am not—
I am not a philosopher.
I have been made
an 'existentialist' philosopher
under force of conditions,
the condition being death:
I will die by a surfeit of flesh.

Five years I have consumed
liquid metals and every poison
to kill off the extra body.
I have killed off my hair,
select parts of my immunity
and the nerves in my fingers.
Now I am told that
the cancer is winning its race to the grave.

For we are all existentialists
when the forward-thinking brain
is blocked
and no plausible future extends,
not a day, not an hour . . .

The body lives in its past,
and when tomorrows end
only the body remains,
dragging behind us,
unable to look forward,
unable to imagine or dream,
nothing to move us
past the last hour on the clock.

All I can think of is the *am—not am*
of going under anesthesia,
and when the end comes,
you won't even know
you never woke up . . .

Even severed only in thought,
the stump of my soul
recoils like a headless snail,
and I am left alone
in a meaningless body,
moving toward a wall
where no one writes their graffiti.

Because there is no plausible
future for the forward
thinking mind,
life dead-ends like a highway
in the middle of an overpass;
one departs without leaving
a forwarding address.

For what is the good
of building castles on the shore,
when the tide
comes at night
and reclaims what it owns—
unless children return
and build them again?

Yet in reality there's really
only one issue
for the dying:
the getting of earthly
affairs in order.

And I am no head-on crash
on a wrong-way highway,
whose last thought
is left hanging;
I have done all my doings
and tied up my loose ends,
except one—
I never found that certain someone . . .

Some people feel
they were born for great things,
and it's funny what things
people were born for,
for others feel
they were born for a woman
they would know
at first sight,
and she would know them—

Still others don't feel it
till glances intersect
in an airport terminal
or subway platform,
then know in an instant
they were meant for each other,
wondering why
they never knew
what was missing before,

someone they were destined
to find,
someone they seemed
to have known in another life,

as if they'd drunk a potion
that never wore off,
an enchantment
that bound them forever.

I can't conceive of a life after death,
and only barely this life—
But I *have* seen a woman's
face in a crowd,
caught her eye as we passed,
felt the thrill of that
person-epiphany—

Some say self-aware consciousness
is an unintended consequence
of matter and energy—
But I swear I have seen a woman
from behind in a crowd,
hair like a flag
among the shoulders around her
and felt I knew her already—

I pitched a tent in the wilderness
and looked at the stars

and heard them saying
man is insignificant—
Still I have seen a woman
lost in thought,
not more than a body
away on a bus,
and was afraid to disturb her . . .

And I looked at myself closely
and saw the atoms
in my hand
and heard them saying
man is randomness,
and told myself I must be mistaken.

These are the truths of our age,
that all take a knee to—
For the powers of science,
we give them fealty.
Yet I have seen a woman's eyes
reflected in a thousand
store-front windows
no science could predict—
and turned to find no one beside me
but anonymous forms.

What is the meaning of relationships anyway?
An old song comes
improbable from the past:

if you can't be with the one you love,
then love the one you're with.

Around me now
night fills with flickering crowds,
the cry of sirens
rails against my ears,
clouds of tear-gas swirl and drift.
I do not think I like that song.

I do not think I like a love
that is not particular,
that can't tell one from another—
I do not want my love
to love someone she's with,
when I am far away.

A shout is given.
The men behind the shields
unholstered their truncheons.
Fear licks through the crowd
like a flash of bait-fish—
Perhaps I was wrong
about the blessings of wrath.

Even inside, the smell of tear-gas
pervades.
I sit in the light from the window,
watch blue and red nerves

telegraph across the walls.
A counterpoint of muffled
cries and chants lulls
like the susurrus of surf
in a vacation rental.
I return here only at night,
avoid tiresome questions.
Sometimes I even doze a little.

Watching the crowds below
I see a frightening consensus,
all are one
in hate of the other,
all are one in love of their own.

Here in the office,
no one hated and no one loved.
Everyone wore a mask,
went home exhausted
and hated their lives.

The Christian in the office
told me all earthly bonds
are dissolved in heaven:
no more banker and debtor,
no more landlord and renter,
no more parent and child,
no more husband and wife,

and lovers holding hands
must let go of each other . . .

If all distinction belongs
to a perishing world,
then fidelity too
must be a perishing notion,
and honor and integrity,
all relationship notions.

Imperishable truths
must start with
imperishable bonds.
Yet we know one another
only a short time
and soon forget
for the rest of eternity.

I leave my keys on the desk,
my ID badge beside them,
write a note for my boss.

Four years I stayed out on leave;
one year I cashed out
my savings,
maxed out my cards,
took cruises,
jetted to resorts,

DAVID CHURCHILL

spent freely in Vegas—
out-lived my money.

Lived in my car
when my apartment was foreclosed,
showered at the Y
till my membership expired,
lived at work
when the car was towed.
Now a new man sits at my desk.

I smell his cologne
when I pick up the phone.
He caught me going out
one morning
when he was coming early;
I was wearing his coat,
my pockets full of
other peoples' food
from break-room
eternally redolent of popcorn.

But it is summer now,
time of long days and warm nights.
I will find a new place
to watch the unrest.
Perhaps I will see
a form in the crowd,
a pair of eyes I know well.

I almost know it now,
the feeling so strong,
the void in my heart is beginning to glow.

I will write a note
to the sanitation department
and pin it to my shirt:
please close my eyes
before you throw me
in your sanitation truck.

Soul-Mate

They went to the mountain
on a week-day in March,
hoping no crowds would be there,
but found the crowd anyway:
parking-lot full,
cars overflowed along the road,
foreign-men walking with their wives,
and a line at the steps.

And the top too—when they arrived,
kids jumping
from boulder to boulder,
running through picnics,
throwing rocks down the cliff—
And where the trees broke,
beyond the throng of
selfie-sticks and cameras,
a vast gray quilt unrolling
under a quilt of matching blankets.

You can see the whole world she said,
when they got to the edge.
You can see the whole world
the other said,
but if you can't see you own eyes,
you can't see anything.

But it wasn't a real mountain,
more like a sack of sugar in shape,

alone among the hills,
and that's what they called it,
the first people who came:
Sugarloaf Mountain,
glad of the rich soil around it.
So they got in line to go down again,
by the craggy steps,
for the wind had come up
blowing cold,
and the sky had grown darker.

I suppose that's true
the first one said:
if you want to see well
you have to know what you're seeing with,
but it wouldn't hurt you
to just agree with me
once in your life.

She did agree but couldn't say it;
she agreed it wouldn't hurt her
to be nicer sometimes.
She thought
something is wrong with me.
It wasn't a new thought.
They drove back to the city in silence.

Probably why I can't get
a permanent position she thought,

have to be content
with temporary appointments,
always an interim.

The best time to find people
ill-suited for life
is in bars that never close
or just walking the streets,
and in used bookstores,
looking for instructions
for something
they can't put a name to—

The best of them find places,
for all that they
choose the wrong path;
that thing they can't name
leads them to itself:

doctors in need of healing
to medicine,
lawyers in need of justice
to the law.

Still—I succored congregations
in crisis when
no one else could,
because I wasn't one of them.

Plato said it first:
God only made one of each thing,
left it to the world
to create its diversity:
made one element
and left it to the weather
to create its snowflakes,
made one person
and left it to the world
to create individuals—

Like the birthday celebration
for a centenarian
of a sprawling family,
a candle for each member;
and when the candles were lit,
a hundred candles
on a cupcake
burned with one flame,
one flame with a hundred feet.

Why am I so impatient?
Do I hate myself too,
who hate other people?
Behind the curtain
we are all one another.

DAVID CHURCHILL

But couples decay
and families pass away,
and the members of a flame
are forgotten.

When the Sunday school teacher
called out sick
didn't I take over the class
instead of cancelling it,
so she could get paid?
And was glad to do it,

and read the children
the story of Genesis,
and said God made the world
and the world was good,
and created people
to take care of the world,
and made them out of the world,
for Adam means ground
in Hebrew,
nothing in us that is not ground,
for we are earthlings
through and through,
and when we die
we return to earth,

and if God had created
heaven,

the book would have said so,
but it doesn't
because He didn't,
but you can still believe
in a life after death,

just imagine an endless series of earths,
and people dying on one
born again on the next,
dying and reborn
like poppies in a field
that always renew,
summer after summer,

because poppies in a field
are all we can imagine
that make any sense,
and earth is the only
place we belong—

And the board got a letter
from one of the parents
and the third time it happened
they fired her.

The reason they fired you
the other woman said,
was because the parents are atheists,

not because
you told their children
there was no Santa—

No one cares about heaven these days.
But you can't tell
the child of an atheist
anything about religion
without getting their consent.

So there you are she thought.
Atheism the religion of the age,
that all bend a knee to—
The golem of science that
serves us, so long as
we don't mind being served by a golem.

She had been planning to tell them
about the origami-birds
of the universe,
folded out of a single sheet
of planets and stars,
so cunningly folded—
they didn't even know what they were.

We are not even born human she thought,
but like animals,
spot-lights of an eternal
now moment,

unreflecting and passive,
for the first blissful years,

until like a mirror
another image is absorbed,
the image of a child with owl eyes,
who suddenly sees
others have eyes too,
and himself and the image
of the others collide—
and the glass cracks.

The elevator reached its destination,
the door opened and closed,
and still she stood there,
staring at her herself,
broken in the elevator mirror,
shattered by movers
with an over-large bed—

and the mirror behind her,
extending the fault
in two directions down a hall,
an infinity hall,
and there you have it she thought,
the soul, a relation of the self to itself . . . .

Then the elevator moved again.

I am half-way not even *in* the world
she thought.
My thoughts are like leaves
in an October gust.
She pushed the button
for her floor again.
This time she got off.

Realities were whirlwinds
around her.
It was as though she wandered
through the galleries
of impromptu museums,

solemnizing weddings
in the bedrooms of houses
where the bride
was pregnant
and the groom wore black
and a little dog at their feet,

and attending house concerts
with two guitars
and a fiddle,
and a crowd in the kitchen,
out-talking the music,

and protest planning
in committee-rooms,

where someone orders lunch
and words appear
on a blackboard
behind them,
you have been weighed,
you have been found wanting.

But always she found herself
before a picture of the sea—
Sea and sky swirling
together in a tunnel
of worldly experience,
the sea eternally empty,
no sail, no ship,
a swirling emptiness
that was almost alive.

It was to this she returned,
treading the silent gallery floors
till she came to the last,
and stood an hour
before the painting,
almost dreaming sometimes
till her face was damp
and her hair disarrayed
by an invisible wind.

The painting was cold
but she was not cold,

standing before it;
the painting was chaotic
but she felt centered,
the painting was violent
but a strange peace possessed her—

Till the voice of a guard came,
waking her in time
to leave the closing museum.

This reality remained
while the others whirled away,
leaving her to return
to the one-room apartment
and the cats,
reluctant rescues of an alley
that spent their days at the window,

to slide a tray into the microwave,
clear off a place at the table
and pull out her notes,
for this was a work night,
the night before Sunday,
the time to set failings aside
and put something else at her center.

Sermon

Consciousness is the water in the fish-bowl
human fish swim in.

Every iota of atoms and
impulse of energy
has consciousness.
We've always known it.
We even have a name for it.
The name we gave it is "Physics"

Nothing could be more unconscious
than rock,
but we are surrounded by rocks
that have been conscious
of rain,
that have heard the whisper of rain
that said follow me follow me,
and have followed it
particle by particle.

Nothing could be more impersonal
than a storm
that harries its molecules
across continents,
calling to the water to rise,
to the ions to mass,
then with a jussive nod
releases its voltage
and sends the water down.

Why have we ignored
this rudimentary consciousness?
The man in the truck
when the lightening contrived
to send a ball through his window
and burn off his eyebrows
no longer ignores it,
but is probably sure
it didn't seek him out personally
for non-payment
of child-support.

The dark lords of creation
that nobody sees
say come in a language
everything can hear,
and everything comes.

We are the origami-birds of
the universe,
folded out of a single sheet
of its gases and dust.
The physical properties
of atoms
contribute to bodies,
the reactive properties
to consciousness,
and it is the cunningness
of the folding

that gives us awareness,
our coming together
that makes us self-aware.

Written this day
from the mountain of self knowing.

Street

People began turning
away from me
even before I stopped bathing—
Foolishly I told
a few friends I was terminal,
then everyone knew.

I got on the elevator
and people
acted as though
they suddenly remembered
they owed me something—

I wanted to tell them I'm
dying, you don't
owe me anything for it,
I'm dying for free—
but I didn't.

I met people at parties
I hadn't seen in a while
who found blanks
in their minds
where my face used to be,
who knew they knew
me but suddenly
couldn't place me.

I have never seen
so many people
struggle to make small-talk
come to life.

I wanted to say I'm
sorry I can't help
reminding you
you're going to die too.
I'm not doing it on purpose,
but I didn't—

The perishing world
is at war
with the eternal now moment,
and I appear
to have changed sides.

Close friends too
are uncomfortable around me.
They pull a long face
like pulling down the blinds,
but I don't
fault them for that.

It is as though
one of their number
has been caught

in a lie,
and they're embarrassed for me.

Friends serve
to distract us from death,
and I whom you
trusted has broken your faith,

for death is taboo,
and dying for any
other reason than
superannuation is a punishment,
and no one knows
what you did
but everyone knows it was something,

like smoking or
drinking too much or
not wearing a mask
and catching covid and dying,
that couldn't happen
to you—

Standing alone
staring at the crowd in the kitchen,
I conducted an experiment:
What if I was the only
human in the cosmos?
Who would I be

and what would I know?
Would I even know
I was human?
Would I even know I was alive?

I *would* have consciousness—
the way a pond
is conscious of the trees
on its banks,
of something blue overhead;

I would be like some kind of magic
candle
that refuses to light—
but would catch fire
when cut into two,

for only then would the petals
whose flower is a flame
bud into existence
and blossom,
because humanity is a plural—

I think now of a stand
of candles
I saw burning in a church,
lighting up a dark
side-aisle with a single glow,

and as I drew closer
I saw some candles were white
and others black,
and still others purple
and others yellow,

yet the hue of the wicks
were all the same,
and all over this country
the flames of candles
are yearning to merge,
from highway slim-jim
and corn nut truck-stops

and endless prairies
and truckers riding jake-brakes
into one-street towns,
past the screens
of abandoned drive-ins,

and the hollows of America
and their prosperity gospels,
and from the cities
of endless suburbs
and disappearing farmland
to the drug-free zones
of inner-city neighborhoods—

And the bodies that feed them,
drawing back in fear,
and the flames in the churches
saying this much we'll merge,
but no more—

we'll not merge
with hermaphrodites nor androgynes
and certainly not
Mohammadans,

and even social warriors
are wondering
is my flame,
that wants to unite
with its own,
safe around these Black lives,
that already have
a claim on my conscience,

a flame identical
to the flames
of these strangers
who have my keys
in their back pocket,
a flame I have no way
to tattoo
or tag or even write
my name on,

and if our flames merge,
will I be able
to get my own back,
as when the hat-check girl
hands you your coat
and you don't notice
the buttons
are on the wrong side,

—and if they're dying,
dying in elevators
or at parties
or in break-rooms at work—
will they pull us down with them . . . ?

And all over the country
people are wondering the same thing.

The inner person
who keeps the candle
from melting
views the warmth of humanity
with dread.

Even lovers can't always
submit to one flame,
but like two horses
shy of each other,
balk at being harnessed together—

How good it would be
to drink a love-drink
with someone you love,
dissolve suspicion and insecurity
and become of one mind,

as in a cemetery I used to pass
every morning and night,
just at the time
when the sun levels
through the tree-tops,

and the stones like tines
in a music box,
that if a giant could wind it,
would play *Fur Elise*,

and as I passed I used to wish
life was like the light
on those stones,

a reflection of something
not of this world
that lit up the dull carvings
at dawn
and left them dark again at dusk,

then returned in the morning,
bringing to new life

the worn names
and their dates.

Two stones stood together,
and a briar
grew out of one grave
and a rosebush
out of the other,
and I imagined they had been lovers,
and their roots
intertwined underground
around the coffins
and each other,
and they were always together,
life after life.

People must be like gods themselves
to live in a world with no god,
but this lack of strength
in my heart

is like a wound that keeps bleeding,
and there is no one
among these gods
who can heal me.

THE SKY IS A GATE

Epilogue

Modern-consciousness man died
on November 29th, 2020.
In the end death came for him
later than expected,
so late it had seemed
death might have changed its mind—

The trees of the city
had given up being colorful,
leaving their claws
upraised in supplication
against a sky that ignored them,
releasing cold rains
and cloudy cold winds
to sweep the homeless
off the streets, leaving
the last patrons of restaurants
to huddle against the frost
at their al-fresco tables.

Modern-consciousness man
was exhausted.
He had outlived his job
and his friends,
his savings and,
shoeless and coatless, his clothes.
He had outlived his life.

He heard a recording of bells.
Steps were before him,
a door, people going in.
He followed them in.

As death drew closer
he had become more obsessed
and with delirious
determination
scanned the faces of the congregants—

As the last sound exhaled
and the church grew silent,
he collapsed in a pew.

From behind, the dark forms
spaced out before him
among the pews
appeared like a black sail,
that as they rose
and sat down and knelt
and stood up,
seemed like the last stirrings
and luffs of the wind
as a sail is lowered
on a ship coming to port,

so at one moment
it seemed the congregation

turned its back on him,
the next that a black sail
was furling.

A woman's voice that both
echoed and was artificially
loud began speaking.

This is how God
brings the world
into conformity with itself.

As the moon rules the tides
and the sun rules
the seasons,
the world has its meaning
outside of itself.

Something eternal
reflects in our seasons,
something that is all things at once
reflects in our changes.

This is how God brings *us*
into conformity,
like metal filings with a magnet,
evil self-limits
and the good enlarges.

Just as God gives
life to its children
and does not take it away,
so do we
give life to our children
and do not take it away.

We live in an Antikythera machine.
There is no part
that doesn't mirror the whole.
The smallest gear
mirrors the biggest gear,
and every gear mirrors
the circles of the stars.
Every part of life
is reflective of the whole.

We exist the voice said
because God exists.
We are one mirror of God,
each one unique
because God is unique,
endless together
because God is endless alone.
We too correspond
to something transcendent.

We find our transcendence
in the world
because God is in the world.

We are like glints of the sun
on waves that dissolve
into spray
in millions of lives,
that no more stay together
than spray stays together,
but with each new dawn
awake scattered and changed,
but never alone,

and our hope is in this,
that because stones
stand on a plain
for thousands of years
and pyramids in the sand,
and because we
make resolutions
and consult therapists
and follow new diets
and turn over new leaves,

so we also have hope
of being able to contribute
to our last

transformation,
the one we call death,

that what we do here
affects who we are there,
and who we love here
affects who is with us there.

It will be like a new ship
that sets sail,
our achievements
will be the sails,
what enlightenments we gained
will be in our parents
and our friends are the crew.

For those who have not received
the gift of faith,
consider gratitude,
which is better than faith.

Faith, gratitude and joyousness,
these are the promise.

Amen the voice said. Let us believe.

Music struggled to swell
from an archaic amp
and voices rose in a chorus,

tuneless and out of tempo.
Then there was a procession
and people began leaving.

The last person to appear
came slowly down the aisle,
a woman in black,
black robe and white collar,
a rainbow-banded stole.
She stopped at the last pew
and lowered her mask.

Ah, dear friend she said.
Is it too late
for two people to die
holding hands?

www.ingramcontent.com/pod-product-compliance
Lightning Source LLC
Chambersburg PA
CBHW021341090426
42742CB00008B/684